Wheels Around Dunoon and C

by
Robert Grieves

CW0407568

Dunoon pierhead in summer 1964. This was the last year of operation for Graham's Dunoon Motor Services, which ceased business on 31 December when the local runs were taken over by Cowal Motor Services. DMS tended to have a fairly high turnover of second-hand buses, which they kept for only a relatively short time. RN 7745 was a 31-seat Duple-bodied Leyland Tiger TS7 which had started life with Ribble of Preston in 1936 and was rebodied, again by Duple, in 1950. It is seen working the Dunoon circular town service.

© Robert Grieves 2005
First published in the United Kingdom, 2005,
by Stenlake Publishing Ltd.
Telephone: 01290 551122
Printed by Cordfall Ltd., Glasgow, G21 2QA

ISBN 1 84033 338 3

The wheels in this scene are represented by those of the horse-drawn milk cart in Sandbank at the turn of last century, possibly owned by Dalinlongart Farm. Customers would bring out their jugs to be filled by the milk boy from the highly polished brass taps on the barrels on board. This view looking towards Dunoon is still recognisable, but at that time the offices and printing works of E. & R. Inglis' *Dunoon Standard and Argyllshire Observer* were to the left. The shops on the right in Oakfield Place are still there, but with new owners of course.

Front cover: At the top of the 'Rest and be Thankful' hill road in May 1964 with MacBraynes No. 164 (HGD 905), one of 22 Duple-bodied Bedford OLAZ type buses purchased in 1952 for rural services. 164 was working the morning run from Arrochar Station to Carrick Castle and after the stiff climb up 'the Rest' has turned on to the B828 single-track road through Glen More to Lochgoilhead. Loch Restil shines in the summer sun, with the main A83 road to Kintyre snaking along its shore towards Butterbridge, following the line of General Wade's military road of 1754. In the lay-by beside the telephone kiosk are two parked cars and a caravan, whose occupants are enjoying a picnic. This of course was long before the present car park and picnic area were constructed in the area to the right of the picture.

Inside front cover: It is 8 a.m. on 3 July 1978 at the Dunoon road end at Auchenbreck, and the first day of operation of the post bus introduced by Royal Mail between Dunoon and Tighnabruaich to replace the unremunerative bus service previously run by Cowal Motor Services. Colintraive postman David Edgar stands ready to load his 1973 Morris 1000 post office van, UVS 968L, with the mail and newspapers brought from Dunoon in KSM 205P, the 1975 eleven-seater Commer post bus driven by John Openshaw who also took the photograph.

FOREWORD

A century ago the importance of the Cowal Peninsula and Dunoon in particular as a holiday destination was much more obvious than today. The popularity of this area continued into the 1950s and 60s with large numbers of visitors arriving on every steamer, many coming from the Glasgow area which was little more than an hour's journey away by train and ferry. Others came from much farther afield, some on organised coach holidays. Sadly, visitor numbers have since declined with the steady increase in car ownership and the availability of cheap flights to warmer climes. This is indeed a pity as Cowal today has probably more than ever to offer the visitor, and all just a short trip from Scotland's most populous area (but a world away at the same time).

Dunoon can claim to have been at the forefront of some of the earliest motor vehicle operations anywhere in the British Isles and boasted one of the first public motor services in the country, several years before the City of Glasgow in fact, and even before Edinburgh's pioneering service along Princes Street. The rather grand sounding title of the firm in question was the Glasgow & West of Scotland Motor Car Company Limited, which was incorporated in Victorian times in December 1897. John MacDonald, a Glasgow-based mining engineer, was in control but there were also a couple of Dunoon shareholders in the business – A. J. M. Bennet, a solicitor, and William Hall, a local landowner. Services between Dunoon and Sandbank started in March 1898, operated with two eight-seat Coventry-built Daimler open wagonettes. A local entrepreneur, Daniel McPhun of Alpine Villa, Sandbank, also began a service over the same route with a similar vehicle but soon fell foul of the law since he operated without the necessary licence from the local magistrates.

What must have been the first recorded accident in Argyllshire involving a motor vehicle took place on 16 March 1898, less than a fortnight after the new passenger service started. One of the Daimlers was turning at the foot of Ferry Brae in Dunoon when it was in collision with Sir Francis Powell's brougham which came along Argyll Street. Fortunately there were no injuries as neither carriage nor motor had occupants, but the carriage suffered a twisted rear wheel and spring and the horses needed to be calmed.

Objectors to the new motor vehicles soon voiced their opinions. For instance, a strongly worded letter of complaint to the *Dunoon Observer and Argyllshire Standard* in May 1898 from someone who simply signed themselves 'Hunter's Quay resident' stated: 'Why the erstwhile tranquility of our charming Highland retreat should be invaded by this unsightly and highly distracting monstrosity passes the understanding of the average mind'. It's perhaps just as well that he is not around today. Even the *Dunoon Observer*, mentioned above, was hardly impartial on the subject as in an editorial shortly after the commencement of a new motorbus service in 1906 it printed:

> There can be no doubt that the motor car is and becomes more and more a social nuisance and plague. Not only does the rate of motor speed endanger life, but it destroys the convenience and amenities of public highways and country roads, while its dust-clouds engender influenza and other diseases.

The paper called for the speed limit to be reduced (it was a giddy 12 mph at that time!). In those days it must be remembered that road surfaces were unsealed and many tended to be dust-bowls in summer weather and quagmires in winter.

Another interesting and little-known detail concerns SB 1, the first motor registration number allocated in Argyllshire. This was carried on an Argyll car owned by Dunoon resident Colonel John Smart Matthew of Bullwood, who was general manager in Edwardian times of the Argyll motor works at Alexandria.

This nineteenth book in the nostalgic *Wheels Around* series illustrates examples of many forms of wheeled transport used in the Cowal district over the years. As usual I must thank all those who freely offered help in its compilation, including Dick Fitzpatrick, Harry Graham, Archie McBride, Ian Maclean, Donald McNab, Cathie Montgomery, Donald Morrison, John Newth, John Openshaw, Bill Polson, Geoff Spearman, Jimmy Whitton and Jack Wilson.

Victorian and Edwardian Dunoon was alive with the sound of horses' hooves in the streets. In the days when motor transport was still in its infancy, the horse was all-important as the main means of hauling carts and carriages on every kind of collection and delivery. Since there has never been a railway in Cowal (despite early proposals), horses pulled the local public transport, such as it was, in the shape of charabancs and coaches, before motorbuses appeared on the scene. Especially during the summer seasons, the many visitors who flocked to Dunoon would take one of several trips that were available – 'Round the Hill' to Ardentinny for example. This photograph of a four-in-hand coach owned by Fraser's hiring establishment of Dunoon Pavilion buildings was taken at the Coylet Inn on Loch Eckside, where a pause for refreshment was made. Their Round the Hill tour was advertised as '32 miles for four shillings from Dunoon pier daily at 1030 via Kirn, Hunter's Quay, Ardnadam, Holy Loch, Benmore Estate, Loch Eck, to Whistlefield Hotel (2 hour break for lunch) then Glen Finart, Ardentinny, Loch Long, Blairmore, Strone, Kilmun and home via shore road, arriving around 5.30 p.m.' The coachmen took a great pride in their profession and in their personal appearance, and were a splendid sight in their grey or black top hats, red coats, breeches and leggings.

Another Edwardian view of James Fraser's popular 'Round the Hill' horse-drawn coach, seen descending towards Glen Finart and Ardentinny. The climb from Whistlefield Inn to the summit was so severe that passengers were requested to walk to ease the load on the horses. The descent to Loch Long was equally steep and, as may be seen, the clients were asked to continue walking with only the elderly or unfit remaining on board. All part of the day's enjoyment of course (assuming the weather was kind). Similar excursions from Dunoon were operated by rival hiring establishments including Henderson of the Queen's Hotel Stables, Kirn (who offered extra luxury with a 'rubber tyred coach') and Alex Baird of Argyll Street, Dunoon. The latter advertised 'landaus, wagonettes, dog-carts, broughams and brakes' for hire and also ran a funeral undertaking business. Baird later replaced his horse-drawn fleet with motor vehicles and became one of the largest charabanc and motor coach proprietors in Dunoon (see pages 18–20).

A view from late Victorian times showing three coachloads of passengers arriving at Inverchapel pier at the southern end of Loch Eck to join the diminutive screw steamer *Fairy Queen* for the 1100 sailing to the head of the loch. This called en route at Whistlefield jetty, from where hardy excursionists

could walk to Ardentinny via Glen Finart and catch the afternoon steamer from Lochgoilhead back to Greenock and then take the train home. The majority who remained on board to Loch Eckhead were met again by horse-drawn coaches bound for Strachur, where they joined PS *Lord of the Isles* for Inveraray and the sail home via the Kyles of Bute to Greenock and Glasgow. The tour could also be enjoyed in the opposite direction. It must be mentioned that probably Scotland's first mechanically propelled passenger coaches operated in Cowal even before Russell's unfortunate Glasgow to Paisley steam coach of 1834 which blew up at Halfway. The honour for this venture goes to David Napier, the famous shipbuilder and engineer, who around 1830 built steam carriages to convey passengers who had sailed from Glasgow to his pier at Kilmun on his own vessels the short distance to Loch Eck to join the steamer *Aglaia*, also owned by Napier. After sailing up the loch, another of Napier's steam carriages would further convey the customers through his Glenshellish Estate and on to Strachur to meet the Inveraray boat. Sadly little is known about these pioneering steam coaches, which formed part of what was the predecessor of the later Victorian 'Loch Eck Tour' which was to continue for well over a century, latterly operated by pneumatic-tyred luxury motor coaches. The often underestimated Napier was undoubtedly a man much ahead of his time.

Below: John 'Starchy' McDiarmid (so-called because he always wore a starched white wing collar) of the Royal Hotel Garage, Innellan, placed regular adverts in the local Dunoon press from the late 1890s for his carriage hiring and funeral undertaking services. He also advertised a regular horse-drawn charabanc service (named 'Victoria') which is seen here leaving Innellan in Edwardian times on one of its four daily journeys (weather permitting) to and from Dunoon. This service had been doubled by 1904 with an additional chara named 'Duchess' supplementing the service. These names were later given to McDiarmid's motorbuses when they replaced horse transport, which was abandoned once the motor age was better established.

Above: This 1929 scene at Dunoon pierhead shows two of 'Starchy's' vehicles awaiting custom for Innellan and Toward. The Ford fourteen-seat open charabanc (SB 2829) has its hood rolled back for passengers to enjoy the sunshine. This vehicle was named 'Princess', while behind it is 'Victoria' (SB 3211) which was a fourteen-seat Chevrolet. Another member of the fleet was called 'Britannia', as it was then the custom to name individual buses, creating a colourful local scene in places like Dunoon where the many transport companies operated a wide variety of different named and liveried buses. In 1934 McDiarmid acquired the licence of John Brackenridge of Innellan who had been a rival operator on the Dunoon, Innellan and Toward service, but only a year later sold out to Sam Crawford's Dunoon Motor Services, a company which was slowly expanding and buying out competitors in Cowal.

The pioneering passenger motor services of 1898 mentioned in the foreword lasted only very briefly in Dunoon, since the two Daimlers of the Glasgow & West of Scotland Motor Car Co. were shipped over to Ayr at the end of June that year and commenced running to and from Burns' Monument, which was presumably considered a more lucrative proposition. Horse-drawn transport continued to reign supreme in Cowal until 1906 when a further attempt was made by motors on the Sandbank service. This time the promoter was Edward Crosher, a nut, bolt and rivet manufacturer in Glasgow whose Cowal home was in Alexandra Parade, Kirn. Crosher purchased three new Scotstoun-built Albion 16 h.p. buses with twelve-seat open bodywork by Penman of Dumfries. They were registered SB 36, 37 and 38, and this view shows SB 36 making its inaugural journey on 13 April 1906, with Edward Crosher alongside driver Alex Urquhart and some local councillors and businessmen in attendance.

The same Albion with the conductor on the running board photographed at the Argyll Hotel in Sandbank (destroyed by fire in the 1980s), with one of McDougall's rival horse-drawn charabancs behind. The destination board reads 'Dunoon & Sandbank fare sixpence', while the fleet name 'Forward' (the town motto of Dunoon) appears above the dashboard and 'Dunoon Motor Service' is painted along the side of the roof. Crosher also instituted afternoon motorbus tours from Dunoon for the summer season of 1906 and was therefore the first to do so. From Mondays to Wednesdays he offered the choice of Coylet, Ardentinny or Toward Castle. This service lasted until Crosher sold the three buses in 1909 to an operator in Largs, by which time other owners' motorbuses were running on the Sandbank service.

Nowadays the mass exodus from Glasgow and the surrounding industrial towns to the once-popular resorts on the Firth of Clyde simply does not happen. Things were very different, however, until around the 1960s, before the advent of cheap holidays to Mediterranean countries. Dunoon, for instance, was for many people one of the best-loved choices for a summer holiday destination. Apart from the Glasgow 'Fair Fortnight' the town's busiest time was, and still is, Cowal Games day – the final Saturday of August – when thousands of visitors provide bonus business for local tradespeople. This panorama shows the esplanade on games day 1926 with the clock on the tower of the High Kirk indicating that the photograph was taken at 12.22. Most of the charabancs were shuttling to and from the games field and since they all have their hoods rolled back the day was at least dry. From the left at the Castle Gardens sign are: a model T Ford car; a model TT Ford charabanc and two Lancias (ES 7378 and SB 2079) of Hartley's 'Silver Line'; an unknown

model TT Ford; Hartley's 1921 Commer SB 839 ('Silver Duchess'); Ford TT SB 1539 ('Silver Lady'); another unknown Ford, with two more of Hartley's Lancias including 'Silver Prince' behind; and yet another Hartley Lancia ('Silver Countess') with a Commer, 'Silver Queen', alongside. At the end of the row is SB 1809, a Vulcan of Baird's 'Royal Blue Line'. Also visible are cars used as taxis (mainly model T Fords) while the leading Ford fourteen-seat charabanc in the right-hand corner is SB 1867 which was owned by Marshall of Dunoon and named 'Boy Blue'. The scene also shows the Edwardian Pavilion buildings which burned down in 1949 and were later replaced by the Queen's Hall. Charabanc proprietors Ernest Hartley and Alexander Baird both had offices in the Pavilion, as did some of the horse-drawn coach operators in earlier years, a prominent position ideal for capturing customers leaving the steamers at the nearby pier.

The name Montgomery of Strachur is important in the transport history of Cowal. William Montgomery was the village blacksmith in Victorian times and also provided horse-drawn hiring, haulage and carting plus the horse-drawn mail coach service along Loch Eck to Kilmun on the Holy Loch, meeting the steamer to and from Gourock. Mails had also been brought by Montgomery's packhorse from Cairndow to Strachur post office in the days when the mail had to be taken on foot over the Laroch to Ardentinny and thence onwards by steamer to Gourock. Progression into the era of the motor vehicle was inevitable and in 1909 Montgomery acquired his first car, an Arrol Johnston dogcart (SB 117), followed in 1912 by a White (SB 197). An open Commer twenty-seater named 'White Heather' arrived in 1913 and was the first motor touring charabanc in north Cowal. Montgomery's horse-drawn mail coach contract from Strachur to Kilmun continued until the First World War when his horses were commandeered for war service, necessitating the introduction of motor mail on this run. The vehicle used initially was SB 197, the White petrol car (painted green incidentally, as were most members of the fleet in the years to follow). In 1921 Montgomery built a garage opposite his smiddy on Clachan Brae and was appointed the Argyllshire dealer for Ford cars. From 1925 a Dodge dealership was also held for a period. This 1922 picture shows the Clachan, Strachur, a year after Montgomery's garage (right) was opened. The cars parked outside are a Calthorpe Minor sports model in the foreground and two Ford Ts beyond. Across the street, outside the smiddy (just out of shot) the front end of the solid-tyred chara 'White Heather' is visible. This had Lanarkshire registration V 2896.

William Montgomery & Sons held the Ford agency for Argyllshire and so naturally they operated Fords in their own fleet of hire cars, buses and lorries. However, other makes such as Dodge and Dennis buses were also used. Montgomery's cars and subsequently motorbuses continued to operate the mail contract between Strachur and Kilmun after their horse coach was finally withdrawn during the First World War, and when the GPO switched the main mail delivery and collection point from Kilmun to Dunoon in 1929 Montgomery accordingly altered his service to suit. From Inverchapel at the south end to Cambusdhu at the head of Loch Eck, the bus driver delivered the mails, parcels and papers. Mail also arrived from Inveraray via the ferry to St Catherine's, where it was met by Montgomery's bus for Dunoon, with additional collections at Glenbranter, Inverchapel Lodge, Benmore gates and Cot House en route. Apart from the mail contract, Montgomery also operated bus tours from Strachur in the days when few folk had cars and were much more dependent on public transport. TMG 843, the Albion bus shown here, was used in the 1950s and 60s both on school runs and on the regular service to and from Dunoon, where it is seen at the pierhead stance. It had been new in 1948 with bodywork by Thurgood of Ware, Herts., to the London Co-operative Society and is remembered as having been the first diesel powered bus in Montgomery's fleet.

The Ford dealership gained by Montgomery for Argyllshire in 1921 was to prove of increasing value as the motoring age slowly but surely gathered momentum. This scene dates from that year and shows a left-hand drive model T, the famous little car which was to ensure immortality for Henry Ford and was one of the first to be supplied by Montgomery. An incredible fifteen million were built during its lengthy production run from 1908 until 1926, and of course this was the car Henry proudly claimed could be in any colour 'as long as it's black'. This particular 'tin Lizzie', as they were familiarly known, was registered SB 1256 in 1921 to Archibald McNichol, proprietor of Dalnacraig boarding house at Creggans. Archie was usually referred to as 'Pierie' since he was also pier-master at Strachur, which at that time was a port of call for pleasure steamers to and from Inveraray and the Firth of Clyde resorts. A third income came from his modest car hire business in an era when Strachur saw more tourists than today, and the model T was used for this purpose. Archie junior is seen at the wheel on the then unmade single track road along Loch Fyneside between Newton and Strachur.

Sam Crawford could probably be regarded as Dunoon's first 'proper' bus operator, with vehicles which had evolved at least a little from the cumbersome pioneering open wagonettes of Edwardian times. SB 1064 was a Siddeley–Deasy with Rudge–Whitworth wheels registered to Crawford shortly after the First World War, in which conflict it had served as an ambulance. It was bought at a war department vehicle sale and converted to carry the charabanc bodywork seen here, painted red and given the fleet name 'Glen Masson'. This early 1920s photograph shows the chara at Dunoon pierhead, where driver Jimmy Garrity awaits custom for Innellan. Jimmy drove for several different bus owners in the 1920s (as was the custom) but many years later in the 1950s and 60s was general manager of the A1 service buses based in Ardrossan.

Archie McBride of Kames commenced his transport operations early last century with a horse-drawn cart employed in general contracting work to and from the old gunpowder works at Millhouse. Later he operated a horse-drawn charabanc from Tighnabruaich to Kilfinan and Otter Ferry, mainly for the benefit of summer visitors to the area. In the early 1920s he succumbed to modernity and bought his first motor car. A variety of second-hand taxis and hire-cars were to follow which were mainly Fords but also included Daimler, Essex, Renault and Sunbeam makes. This photograph is something of a mystery, as no one today is aware of the circumstances surrounding SB 1752, a 1922 model T Ford seen minus its body and hence in chassis form only. Wearing his peaked chauffeur's cap as usual is Archie McBride at the wheel, with several helpers pushing in what seems an attempt to get the Ford started. One of these (wearing the 'Paw Broon' cap of the period) is John Olden, and the background confirms they are on the shore road near Tighnabruaich pier. McBride's cars did good business meeting holidaymakers and day trippers from the various steamers and delivering them to their accommodation or going for a drive. Popular runs were to Ostal Bay and around Ardlamont Point or over the Ballachandrain (Pass of the Thorn Tree) to Glendaruel.

DUS 184 was new in 1944 and one of several Bedford lorries owned by Archie McBride, with others including Albions, Dennises, Seddons and latterly Ford Thames Traders. This picture was taken across the bows of a tractor and shows driver Laurence Davidson beside the O-type Bedford (which was fitted with a Perkins diesel engine) in McBride's premises at Fairfield Garage, Kames. Double-deck cattle float bodies like this were fitted to most of the McBride fleet, whose livery was a stained wood effect with a red band. Close inspection shows the sign-writing to read 'McBride's – Kyles of Bute and Glasgow Carriers'. At the carriers' quarters in Bell Street, Glasgow, one of the dispatchers would shout 'MacBraynes for the Highlands, but McBride's for the Kyles'. On three days a week the lorries left Tighnabruaich in the morning for the long return journey to Glasgow via Loch Fyneside, remembering that the new road to the Kyles did not exist until 1979. Typical cargoes, apart from sheep or cattle, would include a wide assortment of items for hotels and shops, film canisters for the village cinema, flowers, fruit and vegetables, and even the occasional flitting.

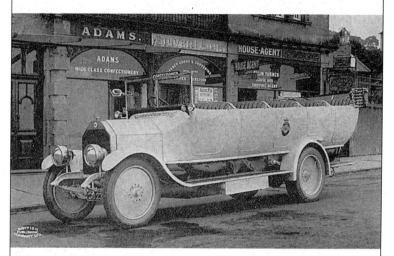

Ernest Goodwin Hartley was a Yorkshireman who came to Dunoon around the start of the twentieth century to teach music. Local newspapers regularly carried his simple advert: 'Pianoforte, music and singing – terms moderate, Ernest G. Hartley, St Cecilia's, Victoria Road'. As the motor age progressed through Edwardian times, Hartley decided the moment was right to invest in a vehicle to operate tours, starting in 1910 with a steam car of unknown make and then a solid tyred Commer charabanc. Service journeys were also initially run between Dunoon and Sandbank and from Dunoon to Innellan, the two most profitable local services, which were covered by many operators over the years. An office was opened in Argyll Street and the 'Silver Line' charabanc fleet was accommodated in a garage in Church Street, with additional space for 50 cars. By 1925 the Silver Line fleet included three Commers, one Lacre, one Alldays, one Reo, two Lancias and four Fords. In later years an assortment of Chevrolet, Bedford, Dennis and Albion coaches was used. Two examples of Hartley's advertising are reproduced here, the one on the left from the mid-1920s SB 852 (lower picture), the solitary Alldays & Onions charabanc in the fleet. The Alldays company had the oldest pedigree of any British motor firm, tracing its ancestry to an engineering concern of 1650! Alldays & Onions Pneumatic Engineering Co. of Birmingham built commercial vehicles from 1906 to 1918 and many were in use with the army during the First World War, possibly including this one. Hartley's Silver Line coaches carried an individual fleet name reflecting their silver-grey livery, such as 'Silver Queen', 'Silver Lady', 'Silver Duchess' etc. and the upper picture on the left features 'Silver Countess' (SB 2348) of 1925, one of several Italian-built Lancia charabancs in the fleet. The advert above shows SB 4496, named 'Princess Royal', a Commer Centaur of 1933. Its luxurious fourteen-seat coachwork featured fold-down tables at each seat and a drinking fountain at the rear.

SB 1389 was one of several fourteen-seat model TT Fords in Hartley's fleet in the early 1920s, a sturdier version of the famous model T and used mainly for commercial operations. This one was a left-hand drive example delivered in 1921, and close inspection of the picture reveals one passenger on the driver's left and two to his right, squeezed together on the front bench seat. Many Argyllshire roads had a restriction preventing vehicles with more than fourteen seats from using them, explaining the prevalence of this size of charabanc. The picture was taken on Loch Lomondside during a Silver Line tour from Dunoon in summer 1922. Many extra drivers were required by all the Dunoon coach companies during the busy summer seasons and quite a number came from Glasgow and sometimes further afield for seasonal employment. Most formed an allegiance with a particular operator, returning annually for many years or in some cases settling permanently in Cowal. It was not unusual for drivers to park 'their' coach on the tours stance at Dunoon pierhead as early as 6 a.m. to claim the best positions!

SB 5085 arrived in the Silver Line fleet in 1936. It was a twenty-seater Dennis Ace with centre entrance coachwork built in Guildford by Dennis Bros themselves. By this time, coachwork had developed from the open charabanc style of the 1920s, but tour operators such as Hartley still specified opening 'sunshine roofs' as they were known. Livery on this coach was an unusual white marble effect, with dark maroon roof and light blue band. All the local rival operators tried to outdo one another with the distinctive colours and luxury of their coaches. When delivered it was named 'King Edward', as may be seen, but on his abdication later that year was hastily renamed 'King George'. Following Ernest Hartley's death the business was transferred to his wife, Florence, and later to his son, Stanley O. Hartley. In 1947 the concern was acquired by former rival coach operator Fitzpatrick of Dunoon along with seven coaches, including this one, but continued to operate under the Silver Line name for a period. In turn, Fitzpatrick sold out to Gold Line in 1958.

Chevrolet SB 3586 was brand new when seen at Glendaruel in 1930. It was the last of this make in Hartley's Silver Line fleet and named 'Silver Duchess', replacing his previous Commer charabanc which had carried this name (see pages 8 and 9). From 1931, Bedfords replaced Chevs and became Hartley's preferred choice of coach. After serving for a few seasons in Dunoon, SB 3586 was sold to Park's Thistle Coaches of Strathaven, forerunner of Park's of Hamilton. The smiling driver sits behind the wheel on what was obviously a fine summer day since the canvas hood has been rolled right back. No doubt the passengers are enjoying a break in the adjacent tea room annexe which, like the popular swing which hung from the tree across from the hotel, no longer exists.

Glendaruel was a popular destination for touring taxis and charabancs from Dunoon, and Bradfield's Glendaruel Hotel played host to day trippers when they called in for refreshments. This scene from 1930 proves the point, with one of Hartley's Lancia charabancs seen on the left and a Baird's Vulcan chara (SB 3329) to the right, with a number of mainly seven-seat hire cars also visible. After their halt in Glendaruel, most tours would return to Dunoon via Glen Lean and Clachaig, completing an attractive circular drive which had set off via Loch Eck and Strachur.

Bell's 'Red Line' bus service was based at Argyll Garage, Alexandra Parade, Dunoon and commenced operations in 1919 with Mr W. Cliff Bell at the helm. Unlike many of the other transport owners in the town, Cliff Bell concentrated on car hire and local route work, but not tours. The main service provided was between Dunoon, Sandbank, then around the Holy Loch to Kilmun, Strone, along Loch Long to Blairmore, Ardentinny and Glen Finart. A service to Benmore Gardens was also operated, which is where the Leyland Lion in this 1935 view at the coal pier was bound (note the supplementary destination board in the window reading 'Cot Inn for Puck's Glen one shilling return'). SC 2942 had been new to SMT of Edinburgh in 1928 with bodywork by Midland (Sword of Airdrie) before passing to Red Line in 1933. Earlier vehicles in the fleet had been mainly Chevrolets and later a mixture of Albions, Dennises and Bedfords followed. Cliff Bell sold his business to the expanding Dunoon Motor Services in 1938, by which time Red Line had a fleet of fourteen buses.

Alexander Baird of Dunoon was already established as a horse-coach operator by late Victorian times. In 1898, for instance, he advertised his daily 'Round the Hill' tour as a 32-mile excursion via Loch Eck and Ardentinny for four shillings, while an eighteen mile round trip to Glen Masson operated both mornings and afternoons for two shillings. Like the other major tour operators in Dunoon, Baird embraced the motor age, but perhaps not so quickly as some since late 1920s adverts still offered horse-drawn carriages for hire in addition to the motor cars. Baird's fleet was based at the West End Garage, Auchamore Road and traded as 'Royal Blue Line' coaches. During the 1920s, Thornycrofts and Vulcans were his chassis of choice, followed by Leylands in the 1930s and mainly Bedfords from the 40s onwards. When the Loch Eck steamer *Fairy Queen* was withdrawn in 1926, Baird's provided the coaching to take passengers from Dunoon on the 'Famous Loch Eck tour' via Strachur and the shores of Loch Fyne to Inveraray, where they joined the new turbine steamer *King George V* to sail via the Kyles of Bute and back to Dunoon in an anticlockwise direction. Baird's coach returned to Dunoon with the passengers who had left the steamer at Inveraray and were enjoying the clockwise tour. With the loss of his job, Tom Blair, former skipper of the *Fairy Queen*, obtained employment with Baird's as a courier on their Royal Blue coaches. Illustrated is SB 5071, a Leyland Cub of 1936 with fourteen-seat rear entrance coachwork by Pickering of Wishaw which remained in the fleet into the 1950s. The driver appears to be encouraging the prospective lady customer to join his tour.

One of several Leyland coaches in Alex Baird's Royal Blue Line fleet was SB 4001, delivered in 1932 with twenty-seat bodywork by Burlingham of Blackpool, a well-respected name in coachbuilding. By this time coachwork had progressed from the open charabancs of the 1920s, but as may be seen this example still incorporated a roll-back canvas section which covered almost the entire roof length, allowing plenty fresh air on fine days. First-class coaches, like this Leyland Cub, tended to operate Baird's longer tours from Dunoon such as Oban or the Trossachs, both of which cost £1. 2s. 6d., which was a fair bit of money at that rather depressed time. Customers would be uplifted at their respective boarding houses and hotels as an incentive to travel with Baird's tours.

Bedfords and Commers were popular choices for both service buses and tour coaches during the 1940s and 50s in particular. Baird's Royal Blue coaches owned SB 7967, a Commer new in 1949 with coachwork by Strachan of Acton, London. Despite the embellishment of twin horns, there was no nearside mirror fitted to this coach! Although admittedly not then a legal requirement, one would perhaps expect it as a necessary accessory considering the many narrow single-track roads in the Cowal area. The photograph shows the coach in 1954 at the esplanade tours stance, with Dunoon's attractive pier buildings behind.

BAIRD'S MOTOR TOURS
TELEPHONE 88
GARAGE ACCOMMODATION

THE ALL-BRITISH
"ROYAL BLUE" LINE
The Cars with the reputation for comfort

20   Baird's advert from around 1930 features one of their Vulcan coaches of the period.

Another of the main Dunoon coach operators in the pre-war era was the Antonelli family. They vied with their rivals to own the most comfortable coaches available, usually specifying particularly individual requirements to the coachbuilder. SB 3577 was a Commer Invader with coachwork by Burlingham of Blackpool, delivered to Antonelli in time for the 1930 summer touring season, but named 'Miss 1940', suggesting to prospective customers that this little lady was ten years ahead of her time. Other female names on Antonelli coaches included Miss Modern, Miss Fresh Air and Miss Amy, this one named after heroine of the air Amy Johnson. Only fourteen extremely comfortable and spacious seats were fitted to the luxurious bodywork of Miss 1940, which could normally accommodate twenty or more. Another special touch was the fitting of cycle type front wings which turned along with the wheels. The Antonellis formed Gold Line tours and the livery was an unusual but nevertheless attractive mix of colours using a greenish gold metallic paint which gave a marble effect, with a green waistline, wine upperworks and black wings. The business was transferred to a company known as Air Industrial Developments during wartime, becoming Gold Line Motors Ltd. in 1958 and finally acquired by Baird of Dunoon in 1968.

GOLD-LINE

PIONEERS OF LUXURY TRAVEL

Gold Line advertisements for 1931 and 1961, illustrating the development of coach styles over 30 years. The one to the left shows 'Miss Modern' (SB 3774) of 1931, which was a similar Commer Invader to Miss 1940 (previous page) but was fitted with Gruss air springs for additional stability and ride comfort. These are seen forward of the radiator and were more usually associated with Gilford buses of the period.

WE OPERATE THE MOST MODERN COACH FLEET IN ARGYLL

DAY & AFTERNOON TOURS FROM DUNOON

booking offices **ARGYLL GARDENS** or **COACH STATION GEORGE STREET**

GOLD LINE
LUXURY COACH TOURS

Gold Line Motors Ltd · George Street Dunoon · Tel Dunoon 1234

A 1961 Gold Line ad featuring GSB 572, a newly delivered Bedford SB type (appropriate for Argyllshire) with Duple Super Vega coachwork.

Opposite: Centuries-old Cairndow Hotel near the head of Loch Fyne in Cowal's northernmost village is a historic coaching hostelry now known as the Stagecoach Inn. Among its guests in former times were Dr Johnson and his biographer James Boswell during their tour of the Highlands in 1773. This mid-1930s picture shows that it remained a popular place of refreshment into the era of the motor coach. The passengers are enjoying some relaxation while their transport peeps around the corner of the hotel as if to say 'No hurry – I need a break too, especially since climbing Rest and be Thankful', for this was a day tour from Glasgow to Inveraray, operated by Walter Alexander, the Falkirk-based bus and coach operator who was shortly to adopt the well-known 'Bluebird Coaches' slogan. Alexander's offered a wide range of both day and extended tours for which they built up an excellent reputation for quality and value. The coach in this view is WG 2352 (fleet No. W20), which was an eighteen-seat Bedford of 1934 with Alexander's own coachwork. It was sold to the Stag Garage of Lochgilphead in 1940 where it provided further service until finally withdrawn in 1950.

Charles Fitzpatrick was an Irishman from Clones, Co. Monaghan, who came to Dunoon shortly after the First World War. Having gained experience of mechanical transport during his wartime service, he easily found employment with Alex Baird of Argyll Street (see page 18), who was expanding his fleet of motor charabancs at this time. After a couple of years with Baird, Fitzpatrick started his own rival motor coach and taxi business in the early 1920s and built the County Garage on Alexandra Parade to house his vehicles. Initially he operated small Ford charabancs between Dunoon and Innellan but abandoned this service in 1924 to concentrate on coach touring. A wide selection of day and half-day tours was soon available for the many visitors to Dunoon, and Fitzpatrick was one of the main coach proprietors in the town running the Azure Blue Line, with Alex Baird, Ernest Hartley and the Antonelli family forming his main rivals. Various chassis makes were used over the years, including Ford, Dodge, Chevrolet, Fiat, Dennis, Bedford and Commer. This view dating from the summer of 1948 was taken at Port Lamont, with the Isle of Bute visible across the waters of Loch Striven. Two of Fitzpatrick's coaches, which had been newly delivered at the time, are seen on a Toward and Loch Striven tour with a full complement made up largely of ladies. SB 6908 was a Duple-bodied Albion Valkyrie which was later sold to Carmichael of Glenboig, while just visible behind is SB 6909, a **24** Commer with Plaxton coachwork. Both were painted in Fitzpatrick's attractive dove grey livery, relieved with two-tone blue.

Fitzpatrick's funeral and taxi-hire fleet makes an impressive line-up along the esplanade in 1947. Leading the line is FGB 645, Fitz's first hearse, which was a brand-new long wheelbase Humber bodied (no disrespect intended) by Charlesworth of Coventry. All the others in the line were second-hand but nevertheless quality cars. The next two are of United States' origin, but date from several years before the American navy arrived at the Holy Loch. JB 8493 was a Packard 'straight eight' seven-seat limousine of 1936, while BGB 375 was a Buick – also straight eight – five-seat saloon of 1937. Behind the Buick comes an Austin Eighteen Iver seven-seater limo, followed by a Dodge seven-seater. Sixth in the row is CSM 555, another Austin Eighteen, then a Buick seven-seat limo which had been owned by Provost Drummond of Greenock. Next is a Wolseley limo, followed by an Armstrong–Siddeley saloon ending the line. Today Dick Fitzpatrick, Charles's son, is a weel-kent face throughout Cowal and still drives his taxi in Dunoon.

Six of the best! In 1933, Sam Crawford & Co. (see page 12) bought these six Albion Victor twenty-seaters, registered SB 4228–32 and SB 4234 with bodywork by Pickering of Wishaw. By this time Crawford and his brother-in-law William Hill had built a garage for the expanding bus fleet in John Street, Dunoon (now occupied by Ian MacCallum's motor business). Sam called the company Dunoon Motor Services, which apart from the final 's' was the same name used by Crosher's early venture from 1906–09 between Dunoon and Sandbank. 'DMS', as the company soon became familiarly known, built up a network of services by means of acquiring a number of smaller rival operators. Routes operated included those to Innellan, Toward and Loch Striven; Sandbank via Shore Road and also High Road; Glenlean; Benmore; Blairmore; Ardentinny and Glen Finart. DMS also inaugurated local town circular services incorporating Upper Kirn and Upper Hunter's Quay. During wartime, ownership of the company passed to the Graham family, who had previously operated bus services in the Kirkintilloch area which had been sold to Alexander's of Falkirk.

26

In the 1930s, when Dunoon Motor Services was under the control of Crawford and Hill, a major proportion of the fleet was purchased new and the products of Albion Motors of Scotstoun were particularly popular. SB 5231 was one of eight new Albion Victors delivered in 1937: five normal control (bonnet type) and three forward control (as illustrated). All had bodywork by Pickering of Wishaw.

A peep inside Dunoon Motor Services' John Street garage in the late 1950s. At this time, DMS bought nine second-hand Alexander-bodied Leyland Cheetahs of 1938 which had originated in the fleet of Alexander, Falkirk. Seen here are WG 7626, newly arrived and still in Alexander's blue and cream livery, with SN 8562 in the DMS red and cream.

The first double deck buses to operate in Cowal were second-hand wartime utility Guy Arabs which arrived in 1949 and belonged to Dunoon Motor Services. These 'deckers were naturally a bit of a novelty initially, with all the children (and a lot of adults) preferring to travel on the top deck. They came from Birmingham Corporation, in whose dark blue and cream colours they continued to operate for a while before receiving the DMS red livery. FOP 356 was one of these and is seen about to depart for Sandy Beach from the former town stance adjacent to the Douglas Hotel (an advert painted on the gable end reads 'Douglas Hotel hot and cold all bedrooms').

This view at the pierhead terminus shows HL 8609, a Leyland Titan bodied by Charles Roe of Leeds, which started life in 1938 with West Riding Motor Services and came to Dunoon in the early 1950s. On this occasion it was working the town local service to Upper Hunter's Quay.

When this photograph was taken in George Street, Dunoon in May 1955, outside the DMS garage, DGB 434 had recently been painted into its new red livery from the green, cream and orange of Glasgow Corporation Transport, where this Albion Venturer began its career in 1942 with bodywork built on a Metro–Cammell framework by GCT at their Larkfield bus works. The advert on the bus is for Strone House, for many years a popular outlet for tweeds and tartans.

in Dunoon

AHF 198 was an ex-Wallasey Corporation Leyland Titan PD1 of 1947 with Metro–Cammell bodywork, which came to Dunoon in the early 1960s. Visible on the tours stance is AYJ 953, one of Baird's Commer Avengers with 'dorsal fin' style coachwork by Harrington of Hove. This had been purchased second-hand from Dickson of Dundee.

Dunoon Motor Services purchased predominantly second-hand buses for its fleet in post-war years, and they came from all over Britain including Birmingham, Bury, Lancaster, London, Middlesborough, Wakefield and Wallasey, as well as from various parts of Scotland. EN 8823 was a former Bury Corporation Leyland Titan of 1946 with Wigan-built Northern Counties bodywork, seen in the summer of 1964 on the shore road through Ardnadam, heading for Sandbank.

DMS bought their very last buses only a few months before the company ceased operations at the end of 1964. They were two Park Royal-bodied RTL-type Leylands of 1950 from London Transport, and had only a brief sojourn in Dunoon, both being sold for further service to McLennan of Spittalfield. LUC 72 is seen at the pierhead stance in August 1964, with the student conductor chatting to a US navy sailor at the bus shelter. The American naval presence in Holy Loch from 1961 to 1992 provided much valuable business for the town, buses and taxis included.

SB 7369 was a well-known Foden in the Dunoon district for several years, mainly because of the distinctive appearance of its full-fronted Scottish Aviation coachwork, built at Prestwick Airport. Initially it operated a variety of day tours for Baird's from delivery in 1948 until the mid-1950s, when it was demoted to the associated Dunoon Motor Services fleet to work stage carriage journeys in the area. It is seen leaving the seafront stance on Alexandra Parade bound for Sandbank via the High Road, passing a couple of Baird's Commer coaches on the tours stance to the left.

Dunoon Motor Services ceased to trade at the end of December 1964, but their former network was immediately continued from January 1965 by Cowal Motor Services, working from Baird's coach depot in Auchamore Road (now Dunoon Builders' Supplies). CMS was controlled by Harry Graham, who had owned DMS and also operated Baird's coach fleet. In one fell swoop all double deck operations vanished and the DMS fleet was replaced by six ex-Trimdon Motor Services Duple-bodied Ford Thames Traders of 1960 (858–863 JPT). Seen in its first week of service with the new Cowal company is 862 JPT, heading towards town along Alexandra Parade on the Ardenslate circular service.

Operating for Cowal Motor Services in the mid-1960s was Baird's 655 JTD, seen here working the Upper Kirn route. This was a Duple-bodied Bedford SB which was sold to Arran Transport in 1967. A major – and to the public very visible – change took place virtually overnight on the demise of DMS and birth of CMS. The abandonment of double deck operation meant no more conductors, with all services one-man operated from January 1965.

Cowal Motor Services' vehicles were augmented on local runs by those of the associated Baird's coach fleet. Seen during August 1966 at the esplanade stance opposite the Bay Tearoom and Baird's original garage premises is RAV 351, a Plaxton Consort-bodied Bedford SB which had been new in 1959 to Simpson of Rosehearty. It was operating the Innellan/Sandy Beach service.

Innellan in 1951 was a thriving community with a variety of shops doing business along the main street. At this time, of course, holidaymakers and day trippers still came to Cowal in their droves. They could even sail direct to Innellan, as the village pier did not close to passenger steamers until the end of the 1972 season, when the final call was made by *Waverley*. After sale to McAlpine the contractor the pier was given a new, albeit short further lease of life from March to October 1974, when it was used as a port of call for vessels carrying workers based at the Ardyne site. It then remained largely unused, and having been badly damaged by fire in 1986 was demolished in the early 1990s. This view of the terrace known as Argyll Buildings looks south towards Toward from the long-since closed Clydesdale & North of Scotland Bank. Parked outside the post office (also long-closed) is CGA 742, a Glasgow-registered Rover saloon new in 1938, while approaching from the distance is a 1930s Lanchester saloon.

Popular paddle steamers *Jeanie Deans* and *Marchioness of Lorne* at Dunoon pier on 27 April 1939, when there was still a powdering of spring snow on the Cowal hills behind the town. *Jeanie* had been built in 1931 for the London & North Eastern Railway fleet by Fairfields of Govan and was probably the swiftest paddler of her day on the Clyde, with a capability of 18.5 knots. She is seen in her relatively short-lived livery of the late 1930s with pale grey hull and white upperworks. After eventual retiral from Clyde waters in 1964, she was sold for further service to the Coastal Steam Packet Co. Ltd. and renamed *Queen of the South*, operating Thames cruises between Tower pier and Southend on Sea. Boiler problems sadly hastened her total withdrawal in 1967. The *Marchioness* was also built at Fairfields but was a year or two younger, having been launched in 1935 for the Caledonian Steam Packet Co. Ltd., with whom she spent most of her service on the Holy Loch runs. She was rendered surplus with the arrival of new motor vessels in the early 1950s and was accordingly then withdrawn and laid up, only to be scrapped the following year. (Graham Langmuir)

Opposite: An isolated telephone kiosk is situated to this day at the 'top of the Rest' where the minor B828 road through Glen More to Lochgoilhead meets the main A83 trunk road to Inveraray and the Kintyre Peninsula. Today's kiosk is no longer of the style seen in the 1930s, but is equally necessary since despite the loneliness of the location it is nevertheless an important junction (and also viewpoint), which attracts passing summer visitors to linger while enjoying the surrounding scenery over Glen Croe. Postman Peter Campbell of Dunoon stands beside EGU 544, his new Morris Eight post office van on the delivery run serving the Lochgoilhead area. This is believed to have been the first motor mail-van in the district and replaced several bicycles. On this occasion in September 1938 Peter was relieving the local driver and waiting at 'the Rest' to collect mail from the big van operated on contract to the post office by Craig's West Coast Motor Service between Campbeltown and Glasgow.

Dunoon master grocer Arthur Blincow used this photograph of his delivery van and shop in Queen Street, at the corner of Milton Road, for publicity purposes during the late 1920s. Wearing his grocer's apron, Arthur may be seen outside his general store which today is Brogan's mini market. In 1929 Arthur married Katie Kent, whose family owned several properties in the town, and a move was made to other premises (now the Sundowner Bar) a short distance along Queen Street where they traded until the 1960s. The Ford van was a classic example of the signwriter's art and acted as a mobile advert for Blincow's grandly named East Bay Emporium, extolling the virtues of 'Challenge' whisky and Whitbread's ales. It was one of the ubiquitous model Ts of the time, and had been supplied through the Argyllshire agent Montgomery of Strachur (see pages 10 and 11). Blincow bought it in 1925 when it was registered SB 2334.

Neil Wilson originally belonged to Carmunnock, between Glasgow and East Kilbride, and served his apprenticeship as a blacksmith, working as such in Babcock's Renfrew factory for a time. After his move to Dunoon in 1919 he continued to ply his trade in the town, but realised that as the number of horses was declining so the motor car was slowly but surely increasing in popularity. Sensing the growing potential of the automobile, Neil managed to obtain the Austin dealership for the whole of Argyllshire in 1922, and a couple of years later built Dunoon's well-known East Bay Garage in Alexandra Parade on the site of a former farm. As business expanded, a Lanchester agency was also obtained and an Oban branch opened in 1934. Diversification into passenger transport came around 1940 when a local bus service was acquired. This was Fred and Duncan Brodie's Sandbank Motor Service, running between Dunoon, Sandbank and Benmore with Bedfords. Later in the 1940s this was sold to Dunoon Motor Services, around which time Neil's son Jack took over the reins of the business. Since his youth Jack Wilson had always been an enthusiastic follower of and participant in motor sport. In 1952 he completed construction of this special competition car for himself in the East Bay Garage. Austin Seven SB 8068 sported an Austin A40 engine, combined with a Ford front axle, and was familiarly known as 'Grasshopper'. Jack Wilson is seen here at the wheel while competing **36** in a three-day Highland trial near Fort William, an event organised by the Scottish Sporting Car Club.

The Cowal countryside is home to many large estates, one of which is Ardkinglas at Cairndow, where the result of a successful day's sport was captured on camera in 1965. Head gamekeeper Willie Manson of Lorimer Cottage, on the left, and keeper Archie McCallum of Clachan Farm, holding the hind's hind legs, seem well pleased. The unknown gentleman to the right, who no doubt paid for the privilege of the proceedings, seems equally happy. The wheels belong to XAU 126, the estate Land Rover, a Nottingham-registered Mark 1 model of 1956 which was virtually indispensable on such an occasion.

Looking along the Loch Eck road in 1934 between Coylet and Whistlefield. At this time improvements were in progress on the previously narrow, winding track which explains the presence of PS 125, a seven-ton Aveling & Porter road roller (built in Rochester, Kent, by the same company which manufactured the steam traction engine owned by Fred Dibnah). This had originally been delivered in 1911 to Zetland County Council, with whom it worked in the Shetland Isles until replaced in 1926 and sold to King & Co., contractors and quarrymasters of Glasgow. King's in turn sold it to another Glasgow roadmaking firm, the National Asphalt & Concrete Co., in whose ownership it is seen in this view of the lochside road prior to resurfacing. These contractors might have had much more work in the Cowal Peninsula if the ideas of Dunoon councillor Daniel Anderson (also sheriff substitute for Argyll) had come to fruition. In 1910 he proposed various tramway systems throughout the county, including two from Dunoon. One was suggested to run via Innellan, Toward, the shore of Loch Striven and onwards to Glendaruel, while the other was equally ambitious and would have been routed from Dunoon via the High Road, Sandbank, Glenmassan, Garrachra Glen, Ballimeanoch and Strachur to St Catherine's. Needless to say, neither reached beyond the proposal stage.

Opposite: The haulage firm of McNab & Weir was well-known not only throughout Cowal, but much further afield too. Based at Garrel near Strachur, their first lorry was Walsall-registered FDH 309, a second-hand ERF dating from 1938 which was bought from Millburn Motors of Glasgow in 1959 and can be seen on the back cover. This was followed by a 1957 Foden, formerly with Adamson of Carluke (OVA 571), a 1959 Albion from Millburn Motors (VVA 832), and then the first new purchase, a 1965 Dodge (DSB 133D). A further new lorry (FSB 105E) was the Albion Super Reiver seen on the facing page, which was supplied through Millburn Motors in 1967 and had one of the early ergomatic tilting cabs, plus a Hiab crane for easier loading and unloading. This photograph was taken when it was brand new and shows Donald McNab (centre) and John Weir (left) unloading timber for pit props at Balmeanach Sawmill in Glenbranter Forest, under contract to Cowal–Ari Sawmills. Although timber haulage formed a major part of McNab & Weir's work over the years, this was supplemented by other contracts, such as the distribution of Marley tiles for Argyll and the isles and delivering drums of oil for Shell and BP throughout Scotland. In October 2004, after 45 years in the haulage industry, Donald McNab sold the business to P. McKerral of Campbeltown, another specialist timber haulier.

'Knight of the Kyles', 'Lady of the Kyles', 'Lord of the Kyles', 'Pride of the Kyles' and 'Queen of the Kyles' were amongst the titles given to lorries in the fleet of Spearman's Transport, Kames. Also, depending on their gender, the message 'At Miles He/She Smiles' was painted across the cab fronts of the smartly turned out grey and red lorries. Joseph Spearman had come to Kilfinan from Haltwhistle, Northumberland in 1929, bringing a chain-driven Albion lorry with him. Service in the army during the First World War had provided Joe with a transport background which stood him in good stead on his arrival in Cowal. A move to Kames in 1934 saw expansion with the purchase of a second-hand Morris Commercial which carried cattle to and from Paisley market. Spearman's operations became part of the Ministry of War Transport unit 11Q24 during the 1939–45 conflict, and vehicles which joined the fleet around this time included three Fordson Thames. One of these, SB 6699 of 1946, is seen in this view with Joe's son Geoff Spearman, who had joined the family firm by this time with brothers Basil and George.

Fodens were favoured in the Spearman fleet and this was the firm's first new lorry of that make, replacing a Ford six-wheeler. It came to Tighnabruaich in 1955 and was named Pride of the Kyles, receiving personalised registration SB (Spearman Bros.) 1120. This view shows it working at MacVicar's Lephinchapel Farm on the shores of Loch Fyne, fitted with a triple-deck cattle/ sheep container body built by Struthers of Jackton. Power was supplied by a five-cylinder Gardner diesel engine. Geoff Spearman recalls that on the uneven single-track roads of Cowal in those days this top-heavy truck tended to roll like a ship on a stormy sea, calling for extra caution from the driver.

Two more of Spearman's Fodens. On the left is SB 496 (originally registered BSB 834), which was a Foden two-stroke delivered in 1956 and named Lady of the Kyles. Parked alongside is BVA 268, the first Foden in the fleet, a 1940 model purchased second-hand from Parks of Hamilton which arrived in Tighnabruaich during wartime. The location is Kames pier, Spearman's base in the Kyles, his garage occupying the former powder (saltpetre) works. Coal was shipped to Kames from Greenock and Troon and delivered by Spearman's lorries to the surrounding area.

Allegiance later switched from Fodens to Atkinsons, and this early 1960s picture at Kames pier shows Joseph Spearman, founder of the business, with two new Atkis. Both carried personalised numbers from previous Fodens (SB 496 and SB 1120) and were named Knight of the Kyles and Lord of the Kyles. Later, in what was to be the company's final decade of business, Scania was the chassis of choice, and in 1989, after 60 years of service in Cowal, Spearman's Transport & Trading Co. Ltd. ceased trading.

Of several haulage contractors based on the Cowal Peninsula, the name Mitchell of Strone is still well-remembered by older people. William Mitchell came from Edinburgh with sons James, John and Alfred around 1930 to settle at Strone, where the family owned a dairy farm and also the village pier. A horse-drawn cart initially served for local haulage work but motor lorries soon took its place – first a couple of Chevrolets, followed by Dennises, before concentrating solely on Albions. A red fourteen-seat Chevrolet charabanc was also owned for a short period then sold to Bell's Bus Service of Dunoon (see page 17). It was named the 'Strone Belle' and sat at the pier with a board in front advertising tours for visitors arriving by steamer. The farm was subsequently sold to concentrate on the road haulage business, which quickly expanded, primarily with the transport of sheep and cattle for Cowal farmers. SB 7674 was one of Mitchell's fleet of Albion lorries, a CX1 model of 1949 painted in the firm's dark red livery, with black wings. As may be seen from the nameboard on the cab roof, a daily carrier service was operated to and from Glasgow, where Mitchell had a small depot. Every journey in those days had to be made the long way round, involving the hill road over 'Rest and be Thankful', since there was no vehicle ferry between Dunoon and Gourock until 1954.

Nationalisation in 1949 brought Mitchell's seven-vehicle fleet under the control of British Road Services. Mitchell's base at Tyneshandon, Strone, was retained by BRS as its area depot and is the location for this view of former Mitchell Albion SB 6234, which had been new in 1940 and was fitted with a four-cylinder Gardner diesel engine. Bodywork was by Mitchell of Greenock (no relation) who were Albion agents and also coachbuilders and provided the bodies on several of the fleet. The regular driver of this lorry was Bill Polson who later became the BRS local manager in Dunoon. Bill's lucky horseshoe mascot is attached to the radiator.

Two more former Mitchell Albions loaded up and leaving Tyneshandon for their daily duties. Prominent is HGD 768, followed by HGD 769, both Albion-engined diesels new in 1950 and both with double-deck cattle float bodies, again by Mitchell of Greenock. The British Road Services name and lion logo was applied to the cab doors and the white letter A against a black square signified the vehicle's attachment to BRS's Argyll division. At the wheel of 'his' lorry is Alex Polson, who was employed first with Mitchell's and then BRS for many years, as was his brother Bill.

In 1963, British Road Services moved from their former premises at Strone to a new purpose-built depot in Argyll Road, Dunoon (now occupied by West Coast Motors) which provided a much more central location. This photograph was taken on the opening day, May 9, with driver Andy Garrity and GSX 408, his 1961 AEC Mercury (Andy's brother Tommy was also a driver). By this time of course journeys were made easier by avoiding the Rest and be Thankful and using the vehicle ferries *Arran* and *Cowal*, introduced in 1954 between Dunoon and Gourock. BRS was the main carrier between Argyll and the rest of the country and the local community was very dependent on the road haulage service for its daily needs.

The old military road can be seen winding through Glen Croe below as two of MacBraynes fleet approach the summit of the Rest and be Thankful hill road in the mid-1950s, en route from Glasgow to Kintyre. In the lead is No. 65 (EGA 642), a Park Royal-bodied AEC Regal of 1947, followed by Maudslay Marathon No. 34 (GUS 411) of 1949, also with Park Royal bodywork. The duo had departed the city at 3.15 p.m. and the Maudslay was the service bus, working right through to Campbeltown, while the AEC was a duplicate only running as far as Ardrishaig. This service had been operated by MacBraynes since 1929, when they commenced it in opposition to the already established Link Lines buses, eventually acquiring the rival business in 1932 and becoming sole operator on the route. Link Lines also briefly maintained a connecting service between Cairndow and Dunoon, but this was not continued by MacBrayne. In 1971 the road transport interests of David MacBrayne ceased, and the Kintyre service then came under the control of Western SMT for a period prior to Scottish Citylink Coaches taking over. They have now been operating the route since 1983, latterly using the vehicles of West Coast Motors.

Lochgoilhead had its main transport link severed in September 1946 when MacBraynes withdrew their venerable vessel TSMV *Comet* of 1905, which connected the village with Greenock, calling en route at Carrick Castle. As a substitute for the *Comet*, MacBraynes introduced both road passenger and haulage services. These were based in Lochgoilhead and provided a bus service via Glen More and what was then the recently opened new Rest and be Thankful road through Glen Croe to Arrochar and Tarbet Station, connecting with trains on the West Highland line from Fort William to Glasgow. Up until this time there had been no motorbus service to or from Lochgoilhead, but passengers arriving there on the steamer and wishing to travel further could hire a car from Alex McEwan (whose family owned the pier). MacBraynes Lochgoilhead lorry collected and delivered goods and general supplies in the locality, and this illustration at McEwan's pier garage shows both the MacBrayne vehicles based here around 1950. The wooden hut on the extreme right was the office of Walter MacCallum, the MacBrayne agent in Lochgoilhead. FGD 4 (No. 76) was a Thornycroft Nippy new in 1948 with fourteen-seat bodywork built by Harkness Coachworks of Belfast, which incorporated a compartment at the back for parcels and mail. The 1947 Commer Q4 lorry was No. L110 (FGA 898). Walking between the two on this wet winter day is Willie MacNicol, who drove with MacBraynes for over 30 years in Lochgoilhead. Initially there was no bus between Lochgoilhead and Carrick Castle because of objections from Carrick residents. MacBraynes therefore purchased a second-hand former army staff car to serve this section. This was EGG 654, a seven-seat Humber Snipe of 1940, which entered service with MacBrayne in 1947 as No. 57. After a year or two the villagers agreed to bus operation, and in 1952 the then surplus car was converted to a pickup truck, continuing to serve the company until 1958.

The Kyles of Bute Bus Co. combined the services previously provided by two independent owners, Archibald McBride of Kames and Colin Simpson & Sons of Auchenlochan, who joined forces in the mid-1930s. McBride's livery had been red and Simpson's was blue; on amalgamation the chosen colour scheme was red, white and blue, with the duo's first new coach painted accordingly. This was GMH 2, a twenty-seater Duple-bodied Bedford WTB model which gave good service to the company until withdrawal in 1954. Local services in the Kyles area connected with the steamers and linked Tighnabruaich with Kames, Kilbride, Millhouse, Otter Ferry and Ardlamont, while a longer run served Dunoon and a trip to Glasgow was made on the first Wednesday of each month, mainly for the benefit of shoppers and hospital visitors. Archie McBride had originally operated a six-in-hand horse-drawn charabanc from Tighnabruaich to Kilfinan and Otter Ferry, later running the motor mail contract on the same route, as well as haulage services, with lorries operating to and from Glasgow. Simpson had initially run a Karrier bus from Ardlamont to Tighnabruaich which on Saturday evenings brought the local folk to the cinema which existed at that time. Representing the Kyles of Bute Bus Co. fleet in the mid-1950s is YJ 8446, a Plaxton-bodied Bedford new to Dickson of Dundee in 1946. It is seen on Dunoon esplanade before returning home on the Tighnabruaich service, which of course before the 'new' road opened in 1969 meant travelling via Strachur. The company ceased operations in the mid-1960s, the services being continued for a period by Chisholm of Kames and then by Colin McColl of Millhouse. Since 1978 they have been worked in a truncated form by the post office mail buses.

Opposite: The short-lived paddle steamer *Juno* approaching Dunoon pier on a hazy summer day in 1938, seen from across the bows of PS *Duchess of Rothesay*, awaiting departure. *Juno* was built by Fairfields of Govan for the LMS Railway Co. in 1937 and was the second Clyde steamer of this name, but was disposed of in 1940 to serve during the war as an anti-aircraft vessel, only to be sunk in the Thames during the London blitz. In comparison, the *Duchess of Rothesay* was a veteran of Clyde service, launched in 1895 at Thomson's of Clydebank for the Caledonian Railway. She served during both world wars as a minesweeper, but on her return from the second conflict did not take up her former duties and was scrapped in 1946 after a distinguished career. On this particular afternoon, *Juno* had sailed from Gourock, calling at Hunter's Quay and Kirn (seen upper left) before reaching Dunoon, and would then continue her schedule to Innellan and Rothesay. Those on board the *Duchess* had been enjoying a Kyles of Bute cruise, returning via Dunoon, then Kirn, before heading homeward across the firth to Gourock and Greenock (Princes pier).

Back cover: Donald McNab of Garrel, Strachur, stands proudly beside his first lorry at Glenbranter forestry office in 1959. Walsall-registered FDH 309 was a second-hand ERF of 1938 purchased from Glasgow dealers Millburn Motors.